Young Writers

POETRY COMPETITION

GREAT MINDS

Your World...Your Future...YOUR WORDS

Poems From North West England Vol I

Edited by Lynsey Hawkins

First published in Great Britain in 2005 by:
Young Writers
Remus House
Coltsfoot Drive
Peterborough
PE2 9JX
Telephone: 01733 890066
Website: www.youngwriters.co.uk

© *Copyright Contributors 2005*

SB ISBN 1 84460 886 7

Foreword

This year, the Young Writers' 'Great Minds' competition proudly presents a showcase of the best poetic talent selected from over 40,000 up-and-coming writers nationwide.

Young Writers was established in 1991 to promote the reading and writing of poetry within schools and to the youth of today. Our books nurture and inspire confidence in the ability of young writers and provide a snapshot of poems written in schools and at home by budding poets of the future.

The thought, effort, imagination and hard work put into each poem impressed us all and the task of selecting poems was a difficult but nevertheless enjoyable experience.

We hope you are as pleased as we are with the final selection and that you and your family continue to be entertained with *Great Minds Poems From North West England Vol I* for many years to come.

Contents

Laura Sanders (14)	79
Chloé Anders (12)	80
Daniel Hoffman (12)	81
Melissa Morris (13)	82
Robert Pickles (12)	83
Martin Pendlebury (12)	84
Rebecca Naughton (12)	85
Adam Nutsey (12)	86
Shauna Amber Rushworth (13)	87
Jamie Hughes (12)	88
Katie Hilton (13)	89
Lee Johnson (12)	90
Alyesha Sayle (11)	91
Rebecca Pyke (11)	92
Laura Atherton (11)	93
Philippa Heath (11)	94
Daniel Haydock (11)	95
Samanta Chan (12)	96
Sam Hughes (13)	97
Isaac Southern (11)	98
Martin Slater (11)	99
Jack Ryan (11)	100
Michael Ashton (11)	101
Hannah Sloan (11)	102
Amanda Young (11)	103
Rebecca Ward (11)	104

Booth Hall Hospital School, Manchester

Emma Haworth (13)	105

Falinge Park High School, Rochdale

Alexandra Kate Bagust (15)	106

Hope High School, Salford

Emma Jones & Kim Watson (13)	107
Chantelle Archer & Abigail Wilde (13)	108
Leonie Marsh (13)	109
Katie Sargeson (13)	110
Ashleigh Vennard (13)	111
Alex Tomlinson (13)	112

Kirkham Grammar School, Preston

Underley Hall School, Carnforth

Walshaw High School, Burnley

White Ash School, Oswaldtwistle

The Poems

Do Not Let Me Fall

Do not let me fall into your arms
If you cannot catch me.
For even the strongest most determined trees
Won't grow through crackless concrete;
And so the seeds
Go untouched
With masked truths and wasted beauty.

If you let me fall
As others have before,
This disease inside of me will spread,
Through every old beloved inch of skin
Until I am dead
While you go on and re-begin.

Please restrain from revealing,
I like you, I love you dear.
When you will forget with passing hours
And concentrate on brighter flowers.
For in my heart I truly fear
I'm already falling.

Tell me, tell me please
To stand back up straight again!
So the winds may blow me
Onto fertile ground, that has to be
Where I can grow openly
And be free.

Promise me darling, promise
Such a place exists,
And I'm not alone in this barren land.
That one day someone will take my hand
Where I need not resist,
The honest, offered love.

I ask you, I ask you
That you may do this,
And do not show me
Any more unattainable bliss.
So for once, dear, hear my plea.
Do not let me fall
If you cannot catch me.

Emma Nutter (15)

Green

Green is the colour of grass, leaves and trees,
Green is the colour of sprouts and peas.
Green is the colour of my sister's eyes,
Who sometimes can be very wise.

Green is cool, fresh and clean,
Green is the colour of a runner bean.
Green is made with yellow and blue,
The green we eat is good for you.

Becky Howson (11)
All Hallows Catholic High School, Preston

The Volcano

The volcano was a fierce dragon waving its arms,
Its voice bellowed and boomed across the smoky air.
Its roasting red hair trickled, stretched and grew as it fell to its feet.
Its eyes gleamed and sparkled with anger watching itself
burn everything.
Its wild legs shrank down to the floor,
And there it was, destroying everything.

Abigail Bates (11)
All Hallows Catholic High School, Preston

Postcard

At first I didn't want to go on holiday
I preferred it in England,
Where I could stay home and play.

But now I'm really glad I came
The weather here is always hot,
Not like England where it would rain

So I'm having a really good time,
Even though I didn't think I would,
And remember the foreign lads are really fine!

Josie Harrison (11)
All Hallows Catholic High School, Preston

Parks

Autumn time is now here,
Summertime has disappeared.
Time to put your woollies on
As that sunshine has now gone.

Children playing in the park,
Laughing, cheering until dark.
Jumping, splashing in the mud
Having fun like children should.

Stamping, crunching on the leaves
Various colours fall from the trees.
Just like snowflakes, they swirl down,
Red and golden, orange and brown.

Children swinging up and down
As roundabouts go round and round,
Climbing frames and seesaws too
There's lots of things for you to do.

Bethany Eccles (12)
All Hallows Catholic High School, Preston

Myth And Legend

I sometimes wonder how life would be,
If there were no tales of wind and sea.
If fairy stories, myths and legends had no meaning,
Reality and statistics have been forever leaning.

For no child will soundly sleep without a good bedtime story,
Have you ever heard the one about the little dragon, Rory?
But what of the creatures of these tales -
Wizards, unicorns, fairies and the hound with ten tails!

My point is of course that these stories didn't come across us
from north west or maybe south,
They were passed on to us through the years
by word of mouth.

Alana Howard (13)
All Hallows Catholic High School, Preston

Black

Black is the colour of the sky at night
Black is the colour that gives you a fright,
Black is the colour of toast gone wrong
Black is the colour of a very sad song.

Black is the colour of Victorian times past,
Black is the feeling when you come last.
Black is the colour of a piece of coal
Black is the colour of a very deep hole.

Black is a colour we see every day
Black is the colour that can affect what we say,
Black is a colour we may not like,
But black is around us, so it must be alright.

Matthew Baker (12)
All Hallows Catholic High School, Preston

Girls

Girls are girls, and
We love our pearls.

We shop till we drop
To find an expensive top,
In confusion
Or even in fusion!

It could be Playboy
It could be Playgirl,
Come on, give us a twirl!

It's usually straight hair
Frizzy, if you dare.
As long as I look good
I don't really care!

Make-up's important in a girl's world,
So that's why my eyelashes are always curled.
Belts are in fashion,
So that's why they're my passion!

So that's why . . .
Us girls are girls!

Jessica Calvert (12)
All Hallows Catholic High School, Preston

My Cat

My cat plays as rough as bark,
He sleeps all day long on the couch
He plays with his toys and me.
He catches mice and brings them back,
He eats all his food from his bowl
But at the end of the day, he comes up to me and cuddles me.

His fur is as silky as silk,
His eyes reflect in the dark.
He pounces and leaps as he plays
In the leaves and he climbs like a
Monkey through the trees.
He's always looking for trouble
But at the end of the day, he comes up to me and cuddles me.

He doesn't stay out very long,
He's more of a house cat to me.
We got him from a farm
He's a half wild thing.
At first he was scared
But now he's as brave as can be
And at last but not least,
His name is Jasper and he belongs with me.

Angelica Wright (12)
All Hallows Catholic High School, Preston

My Poem

It's a bright sunny day,
The sky's so blue,
The grass so green,
The trees so tall
Bad excuse for the flu!

It's a bright sunny day,
Everybody gasping for shade.
Suddenly, the drink's popular
Make it lemonade!

It's a bright sunny day,
It's a bright sunny day.
There's nothing else to say,
Except, 'Everyone play!'

Ryan Creeney (12)
All Hallows Catholic High School, Preston

Girls' Night Out

C'mon girls, it's time to party!
Get on your sparkly shoes,
We're gonna get you in the mood.
The club is where we're going tonight,
We can chat up all the boys in sight,
Never mind how much it's gonna cost,
Dad will pay for what it costs,
Dancing, partying to the club beat.
At the cinema, make sure we get a good seat.
What film will we watch?
It's up to you!
How about Princess Diaries 2?

Laura-Kate Howarth (12)
All Hallows Catholic High School, Preston

Hallowe'en

It's October 30th next week,
Hallowe'en is coming fast.
Pumpkins are on shop shelves, everywhere
And there are lots of spells to be cast.

As the night finally arrives,
Witches fly on their brooms out to fright.
Everyone's in their costumes,
It's going to be a long trick or treat night.

Kelly Lenehan (12)
All Hallows Catholic High School, Preston

Autumn Is Here

Autumn is here!
Leaves are falling on the ground
Making such a lovely sound,
Crunch, crunch, crunch!

Autumn is here!
Squirrels searching for some nuts.
What a lovely sound,
Munch, munch, munch!

Autumn is here!
Hedgehogs prepare for the cold season.
Making such a delightful sound,
Snuffle, shuffle, snuffle!

Autumn is here!
The wind rustles through the trees.
Making such a haunting sound,
Whisss, whissss, whisssss!

Michael Orford (11)
All Hallows Catholic High School, Preston

Daydream

Lessons are so very boring . . .
I'm above the clouds! I'm soaring!
Algebra is so very dull . . .
I'm in Spain! I'm fighting a bull!
Sir's voice is so very dreary . . .
I'm writing a book with Terry Deary!
Diameter! Oh, no thanks!
I'm - 'Are you listening over there?'
You don't want to cross Mr Hanks,
Better get back to work!

Aimée Jane Callander (11)
All Hallows Catholic High School, Preston

Flowers

Tulips and roses
Yellow or red,
All together in a flower bed,
I grew them all to give to you,
But now they're dead and
I'm feeling blue!

Jennie Sugden (11)
All Hallows Catholic High School, Preston

Moving House

Goodbye old house
We loved you so
Fond memories of you
As we have to go

Our lives are in boxes
Inside the lorry
Now we need to go
We are very sorry

Hello new house
Your welcome is warm
Boxes coming in the door
Create a family thunderstorm

Cards on the mantlepiece
Flowers arranged in vases
Mum's casserole
And champagne in glasses

The ringing of the doorbell
And the opening of the door
A warm welcoming gesture
From all at 44!

Nichola Campbell (11)
All Hallows Catholic High School, Preston

But You'll Be . . .

When it's nine o'clock
We'll be going to school
On the cold winter mornings
What will you be doing -
Paperwork?
Oh no, you'll be laid in bed
Only just yawning.

When it's half-past ten
We'll be playing football
In the freezing cold.
But what will you be doing -
Hard work?
Oh no, your office is probably
Growing mould.

When it's twelve o'clock
It's dinner time here.
Either tinned carrots or a can of peas
At this time
What will you be doing?
Not eating!
Oh no, you'll be sunning
On one of your balconies.

When it's two-fifteen
We're out for break again
Warmer, but a lot damper.
But what will you be doing?
Will you be on the phone?
Oh no, you'll be in the sun
Probably being pampered.

When it's three-fifteen
We all run to the cloakroom
We're going home for tea
But what will you be doing?
Not eating fish and chips!
Oh no, you'll be drinking champers and
Cruising softly on the sea.
That's what you'll be doing!

Andrew Hawarden (12)
All Hallows Catholic High School, Preston

The Staffroom Door

Have you ever wondered what goes on behind the staffroom door?
The amazement and wonderment, just behind the staffroom door!
I'm creeping down the corridor, just outside the staffroom door,
I'm halfway down the corridor, just outside the staffroom door.
My hand is on the handle now, the handle of the staffroom door -
Now I push and open the door, I look behind the staffroom door.
A flash! A bang! A shout! A scream! And then . . .
I'm creeping down the corridor . . .

Michael P Graysmark (11)
All Hallows Catholic High School, Preston

What's For Tea, Mum?

As I walk home from school I try to shed some light
On what will appear on my dinner plate tonight.
For starters, I'd like melon with juicy red cherries,
Plump fresh prawns off the North Sea ferries.
Maybe devilled kidneys, hot and spicy,
Or pâté on toast would do me nicely.

My favourite is salmon with tartar sauce,
It had best be that for our main course.
Baby new potatoes with fresh yellow butter,
Take away the peas, they're only clutter.
Golden corn, still on the cob,
Fresh from the pan and into my gob!

On to the pud, my favourite part,
Fantastical cakes, a work of art.
Steamed syrup pudding in the centre of my plate,
Drowning in custard and tasting great.
A cocktail of confectionery, a sweet tooth's delight,
This is what I'm hoping is in store for me tonight.

Who am I kidding? That's not for me!
It's beans on toast or egg and chips; that's all I'll get for tea!

Abigail Carroll (10)
All Hallows Catholic High School, Preston

Manchester United

The best team in the world,
the best players, ever.
Known as the Red Devils,
they're never beaten, never!

Tim Howard, a legend of goalkeeping,
from left to right he keeps on leaping.

Gary Neville, Philip Neville, surely true Reds,
amazing with their feet and brilliant with their heads.

Mikael Silvestre, a great defender,
Quinton Fortune, he'll tackle you pretty soon.

Ryan Giggs gone down in the history of the club,
Ole Gunner Solksjaer comes on as a sub.

Cristiano Ronaldo, twinkle toes
Paul Scholes will defeat all foes.

Ruud van Nistelrooy, the amazing striker,
Louis Saha, hair like a tiger.

The game has started, what happens next?
Sir Alex Ferguson sends a text.

Who to? But the manager of City,
it says, 'We've scored, what a pity!'

By half-time, out come the Reds
thoughts of winning stuck in their heads.

But City got one back, are they in with a chance?
No not at all, they're not France!

Cristiano Ronaldo, running down the wing
with his amazing feet, he can do almost anything.

Goodness United got another!
This time from Gary, a Neville brother.

There's the whistle, it's 4-1!
Ronaldo said, 'Hey, that was fun!'

United have won the Premiership,
but then Howard said, 'I need a kip.'

Silvestre and Fortune, jump up and down,
Philip Neville acting like a clown.
Ruud, Louis or Ole didn't score a goal
but they're not bothered, they put in
their heart and soul!

Amanda Whitehead (11)
All Hallows Catholic High School, Preston

My Friends

I love my friends
they are so cool,
I met them all at primary school.

I've got new ones now,
with my old one's too.
they're always there,
when I'm feeling blue.

Here we are, I'll give you a clue,
this is what we love to do.
Shopping! The hottest clothes in town,
sleepovers! The best gossip around.

Mobiles, make-up and lots, lots more,
if you really wanna know,
you'll have to explore.

So that's my pals,
I hope you like them too,
if you're ever stuck
just ask them what to do.

Rachel Cook (11)
All Hallows Catholic High School, Preston

The Wind

The wind it rippled through my hair,
It whistled through the trees.
It caught my thoughts and carried them away,
Far, far away with the breeze.

The wind it muttered and whispered a song,
It chanted mysteriously.
It swirled around like a rhythmic dance,
Far past the hills and beyond the trees.

The wind, fierce and angry,
Whipped any objects in its way.
It tore through village, city and town.
It sneaked through windows
And tore trees down.
It lashed and swept all day, all night,
It angrily ran far out of sight.

The wind it was gone, gone away somewhere,
The pleasant breeze had gone.
The rhythmic dance, danced no more.
It did not angrily slash and roar,
The wind had gone and was no more.

Katie Drew (12)
All Hallows Catholic High School, Preston

My Tomorrow

Monday
I stood waiting in PE
My heart was racing, my hands sweating
'Jenna, Sarah and Macy!'
Surprise, surprise, picked last again.

Well there's always tomorrow.

Tuesday
We all got ready for rugby
Tears glistened in my eyes
'Emma, Vicky and Naomi!'
Surprise, surprise, picked last again.

Well there's always tomorrow.

Wednesday
Today we're doing football
I sighed, my legs felt like jelly
'Matthew, Nicola and Paul!'
Surprise, surprise, picked last again.

Well there's always tomorrow.

Thursday
We all stood round the hockey pitch
I felt more alone than ever
'Leanne, Zoë and Bex Fitch!'
Surprise, surprise, picked last again.

Well there's always tomorrow.

Friday
This is it, today's the day.
My friend Abigail is picking
'Louise, Natalie and Faye!'
It really hurts to be picked last again,.

I guess my tomorrow will never come.

Danielle Roe (11)
All Hallows Catholic High School, Preston

Amnesia

He's a lone, ruthless warrior,
Lost is his soul,
Where he's going, no one knows.

His life must be dreary,
No memories to live for.

He's an unprotected, fragile creature,
Little to exist for.
No one to turn to.

His life must be dreary,
No memories to live for.

How can he thrive?
How does he cope?
So lonely!

He is alone.

Nichola Hargreaves (11)
All Hallows Catholic High School, Preston

Emotions Of Emotions!

H ope is a forlorn belief, lonely you see,
O n top of a hill longing to be free.
P raying that it could one day fly
E ver longing for an eternally happy life.

F aith is trust, day by day, night by night
A n emotion, nervous, given a fright.
I n itself wants to be popular, noticed
T rustworthy, helpful and charitable.
H ow faith wanted to be known.

D reams are visions, mixed up thoughts,
R aging, lost battles of which you fought,
E ngraved inside your mind, forever . . .
A s we plead, they cry, 'Never!'
M uch as we try but try as we might,
S o they will stay there, we shed no light.

L ove is fatal, harsh but gentle, caring,
O ver the valley, orphans are staring
V ery much looking at their dreams,
E verlasting, they are broken seams.

Gabrielle Rice (12)
All Hallows Catholic High School, Preston

My Best Friend

The sun in my eyes
The wind in my face
The sea on my right
The sand on my left
The speed is exciting
The power of my pony
As we gallop for fun.

Charlotte Woodruffe (11)
All Hallows Catholic High School, Preston

Anger!

Anger is a bomb ticking 10, 9, 8, 7, 6, 5, 4, 3, 2, 1,
Then you explode and do something bad.
When all the mad anger's gone,
Then you are left, feeling sad.

Anger is the colour red,
Red is a colour, dark and bold.
It goes straight to your head,
Must be a sign of getting old.

Anger is a blazing fire,
The flames in your head burning fierce and bright,
The fire gets higher and higher,
You lash out with all your might.

Anger is a streak of lightning,
Flashing like a pointed fork,
You may think it's very frightening,
People watch you like a hawk.

Georgina Vokes (11)
All Hallows Catholic High School, Preston

Why?

The gruesome green eyeball gleams jealously at me,
Its stained, blotchy, bloodshot pupil is eager to kill
Another day passes, another victim dead
Why this way, oh why?
I shouldn't have created this evil, gruesome eyeball
And brought it to life
Its stained, blotchy, bloodshot pupil is trouble to the Earth
All it ever does is stare into a living eyeball
And *wham* the victim is dead.
Why this way, oh why?
Professor Bones plodded into my Chinese takeaway
Minding his own business and ordering his favourite dish
All he ever did was look down in his dish
And *wham* he was dead!
Why this way, oh why?
Only I can look at this gruesome green eyeball
Without facing the awful outcome
Everyone else has to suffer the pain
And torture of the bloodshot pupil
So look out for this evil creation
Or maybe *wham* you'll be . . . dead!

Rupy Burchall (11)
All Hallows Catholic High School, Preston

When I'm Old

(Inspired by 'Warning' by Jenny Joseph)

When I get old, I'll be different,
I won't have a zimmer frame,
I won't live in a stinky home,
Or behave like a snob or a dame.
I won't do knitting or bingo
I will not eat veg or bread.
I'll go around with my walking stick
And bonk people on the head!
I'll eat junk food - pizza and chips,
I'll boogie and dance.
When I'm told to behave
I'll sing and shout and prance!
I'll run around in my underwear
And I'll do loads of dodgy deals.
When I'm old!

Shannen Potter (12)
Balshaws CE High School, Leyland

Think About Me!

Drooping tail,
Frightened eyes,
On this night
I do despise
All the bangs,
Hurt my ears,
Think about me!
While you're enjoying
Your bright display.
Think about me
All locked away
Barking crazy
No one hears
Think about me!

Sarah Bell (13)
Balshaws CE High School, Leyland

Through Clouded Eyes

It's a feeling
In my soul,
Like a memory, yet
So distant . . .
My eyes cannot focus.

It's something that words
Cannot explain.
It's a vision that has no meaning
Why do I remember . . .
An image through the mist?

That sound . . .
I see stone walls filled with
Mystery; shadow dances in light.
I want to see that place again . . .

I can feel voices of past lives,
Beckoning me. I want to return.
I belong behind the iron bars
A pale light through my window
Silence, telling all.

For once I want to sit
With cold, bare arms, in that room
Again, I've waited
I've watched you forever . . .
Through clouded eyes.

It's a feeling . . .
In my soul.
Like a memory, yet
So distant . . .
My eyes cannot focus.

Heather Lythgoe (13)
Bedford High School, Leigh

The Sunset In Santorini

The sunset in Santorini,
Happens every day.
Bright, beautiful and big
As it sinks,
As it falls, like a waterfall.
Makes me drift off somewhere,
Like I had no care in the world.
The sunset in Santorini
Reminds us that we can never be more beautiful.

Alex Hunter (11)
Bedford High School, Leigh

Shadows And Anguish

Tortured anguish fills my ears,
Death and despair is all I hear.
Determined chants follow me,
My vision blurred; I cannot see,
I am lost
But not gone,
On and on I try to run.

Their perpetual droning drives me on,
My body is chilled; am I gone?
Whilst I carry on hoping to be saved,
I reach a huge, glittering cave.
A bitterly cold pain engulfs my entirety,
A black shadow creeps towards my still body.
It moves over me in a watery way,
I am lost,
But not gone.

I awaken
Try to run,
They catch me,
They've got me!
I am lost!
I am gone.

Kristopher Lee (14)
Bedford High School, Leigh

Metaphorical Poem On Me

I am the colour pale blue, in the bright night sky,
I am a timid rabbit scampering across the meadow.

I am the country, Spain, sunny and full of life,
I am the flower rose, beautiful and sweet-smelling.

I am a jam tart, sugary and sweet
Ready to burst my jammy taste.

I am a lullaby, soft-sounding,
Calm and patient.

I am the character of Anne of Green Gables,
Funny and outgoing.

Shauna Sims (11)
Bedford High School, Leigh

My Metaphorical Poem

I am the colour blue
cool and laid back,
I am a jaguar
fast and speedy.
I am the city of Manchester
busy and exciting,
I am the flower, dandelion
wild and sunny.
I am the food pizza
nice and popular,
I am a rock song
fast paced and cool.
I am the person 'Bam Margera'
daring and funny.

Jay Reynolds (12)
Bedford High School, Leigh

A Metaphorical Me

My colour is red
Cheerful, joyful and happy.

My flower is a rose
Beautifully scented and also sweet.

My country is Spain
Warm, bright and also talented.

My food is a jam tart
Sweet, good enough to eat.

My animal is a fish,
Swimming in the deep blue ocean.

My song is Girls Aloud; Love Machine,
Got a fast rhythm and I'm a love machine!

Chloe Pedley (12)
Bedford High School, Leigh

A Metaphorical Me

I am the peaceful colour lilac
of a secret place,

I am the feisty cat that prowls
in the midnight silence.

I am the lively country Malta
that buzzes with heat and
clear blue seas.

I am the beautiful lily of a
secret garden.

I am the sweet passionfruit
from an exotic country.

I am the fun, exciting song
'Saturday Night'.

I am the friendly and kind
'Ally Love'.

Lucy Fleming (12)
Bedford High School, Leigh

My Metaphorical Poem

I am the colour pink
because I'm bright and lively
I am the animal, dolphin
because I'm calm and soothing
I am the exotic Goa
because I like beaches
I am the flower rose
because I like roses
I am the food pasta
because it's good and healthy
I am the song 'Babycakes'
because I am lively
I am Harry Potter
because I like magic.

Charlotte Stout (11)
Bedford High School, Leigh

The Secret Window

The secret window
Has never been seen
Strange, dusty and cream
Small as a star
Different unlike anything
It mesmerises me
Like a statue
The secret window
It's mine!

Rachel Kirkham (12)
Bedford High School, Leigh

Me!

I am the colour orange
Bright and cheerful like a jaffa ready
to burst its juicy contents.

I am a dog
Active and intelligent like a
tiger hunting its prey.

I am a Cape flower
Bright at day, tired at night, like the sun
rising and setting.

I am the food spaghetti
Fidgeting around like a ferret
in a bag.

I am the country USA, Hollywood
Loud, active, love acting like a mouse
trying to make itself heard.

I am the song 'Feeling Fine'
Giddy, like a bouncy ball that never
loses its bounce.

I am 'Vicky Angel'
Daring and dangerous, like a chick
attempting to fly.

Hannah Louise Collier (12)
Bedford High School, Leigh

My Personal Poem

I am the lilacy-blue, in the misty sky,
I am a fish swimming through the shadowy water.
I am the bright daffodil, growing in the spring sunlight,
I am an empty beach which no one bothers to visit much.
I am an apple which thuds to the ground, as it breaks free from
the tree's grasp,
I am the song 'Complicated' by Avril Lavigne,
My life is sometimes complicated and tiring.
I am 'Ally' who is in her own books, she likes to be with her friends.

Suzanne Prescott (12)
Bedford High School, Leigh

Beauty

Beauty is how you behold,
More than silver, more than gold.
Beauty is how you greet
The everyday people that you meet.
To some, beauty is within their voice,
But beauty isn't a natural choice.
Why would anyone want to be Miss World?
To be judged by the way your hair curled!

Paige Alexandra Wilkinson (12)
Bedford High School, Leigh

The Big Fence

The big fence -
It is a metre long,
It is silver and shiny.
Strong, high and protective,
It is like a tower touching the sky.
So protective, you will never be touched.
I feel safe and strong,
I feel like I'm standing behind a big strong giant.
The big strong fence . . .
Makes me feel like I just can't walk on.

Amy Gildart (11)
Bedford High School, Leigh

The Shadow

The night was bitterly cold,
The stars glittered in the sky.
A blurred black shadow was creeping across a wide stretch of land,
Determined to taunt and threaten innocent people with its chanting
of perpetual drowning.
Its presence alone was torture.
Those who witnessed its frightening chill
were destined to a watery grave.

Christopher Bent (14)
Bedford High School, Leigh

Homeless

Walking along the glittering snow,
My eyes become watery from the bitter cold.
I walk and walk over the chilled snow,
My feet have become numb and my hands frozen, all from the cold.

I pass a few houses all ready for Christmas,
Wishing I was back home for the special celebration.
All families come together for Christmas,
But I'll be on my own for this celebration.

The forest is in my glance, the treetops all white,
I declared this time I would walk through the woods.
I felt my face change colour from pink to white,
I remembered the stories of these woods.

My eyes start to blur
As I rush through this nightmare.
Tripping over sticks and stones, I can't see with this blur
It's worse than I imagined, much worse than a nightmare!

At last I see lights,
This terrible ordeal is coming to an end.
In my sights I see flickering lights,
Not my house of course, that nightmare will never end.

Emma Kelly (14)
Bedford High School, Leigh

Hallowe'en

There once was a small bunch of witches
Who told jokes that had people in stitches
They brewed up some verses
Instead of mean curses
That would normally give you the itches
All the goblins got a bad case of the giggles
All the black cats' tails had the wiggles
The jokes were so funny
They brought in lots of money
I wish I'd thought of those riddles.

Ciara Melville (14)
Bedford High School, Leigh

Undiscovered World

Every morning,
every sunrise,
every daybreak
lies an undiscovered
untouched world.
The shimmering sun emerges into the sky,
sunlight uncovers glistening greenery,
golden fields gape wide open,
animals of the Earth awaken,
their eyes open to opportunities,
brains reflect, contemplate
and ponder new ideas.

Holly Rothwell (14)
Bedford High School, Leigh

The Thing

Fear, anguish, darkness, the beast crept,
Still I stood, waiting.
I must leave, it cannot get me, I must run.
The perpetual droning nearing, louder, louder,
I must run.
The watery tunnel ahead glistened
Beckoning unto me.
Light, nearing my sight,
I cannot be caught,
I must run.
The threat of this 'thing' had been declared
Its ghostly arm rested upon my shoulder,
My time was up.
I'd lingered too long,
I cannot run!

James Wilding (14)
Bedford High School, Leigh

Winter's Day

It was a bitterly cold morning
the last bits of snow were glittering in the frosty sunlight.
My blurred watery vision caught a glance of the dark morning sky,
it was like a black shadow creeping on us.

The perpetual droning of the other pupils wide eyed,
declared the tortured chill of the November morning.

The cold was taunting us determined to wake us up,
as we entered the schoolyard, we all did the same chant
of the dreary feeling of another frosty November morning.

We all stood around in unison,
the small white clouds of cold breath rising like a train.
Sleepy-eyed, we all murmured to each other, half asleep
many people ignoring each other.

The cold, dark school building stood over us like a grey prison,
the grey blinds in the windows reminded me of metal bars
and the large door was the entrance to the frosty cell.
The drill bells sounded, we approached and entered.

Scott Hardman (14)
Bedford High School, Leigh

The Greyhound

The greyhound is fast,
Never seen slow,
The hare is running,
Go, go, go.

The greyhound's chase has begun,
As fast as they can they will run,
Sprinting along the sandy track,
Almost as fast as a bullet from a gun.

No pace lost throughout the pursuit,
Carry on chasing they still sprint,
What a great determination,
In their eyes you can see the glint.

Nearing the climax of the race,
Touching towards the finish line,
There is a burst up in pace,
Many would say victory is mine.

Number 2 is the winner,
Flourishing in all its glory,
This is wrong I would say,
Because the hare is the only winner in this story.

James Bellis (14)
Bedford High School, Leigh

My Favourite Football Player

My favourite football player,
He's part of a great team,
Great, talented and skilful,
As strong as a weight lifter,
As skilful as a golfer,
I like it when he takes people on with his skill,
It makes me feel really jealous,
Like I'm going to kill him and take his place,
He is the best player in the world.

Matthew Whitehead (11)
Bedford High School, Leigh

The Slushy Sea

The slushy sea,
It is sometimes smooth and sometimes rough,
Blue, salty and soothing,
As blue as the sky,
As soothing as a bath,
It makes me want to go to the beach,
Like on holiday,
The slushy sea.

Chantelle Pendlebury (11)
Bedford High School, Leigh

The Wavy Sea

The wavy sea,
There are a lot of creatures which live in the sea,
The sea is salty, dark blue waves,
Which sway side to side,
The sea is as blue as the sky,
The sea is as big as the world,
It makes my stomach rumble because
Of the salt in the water,
It makes me feel rough like a storm
As the angry waves go by,
It makes me feel like the waves in the sea.

Daniel Carroll (11)
Bedford High School, Leigh

Portrait Of A House

The road is not a busy place,
Around my street,
It's a long straight road,
There's hardly anybody there.

It's a red and brown brick house,
It was made in the 1930s,
With a small front garden,
And with a big back garden.

When you open the door,
You will see the stairs.

On the right, you will see the lounge,
In the lounge you will see baby's toys,
All over the floor,
Also on the floor, you will see a dint,
Near the door.

Matthew Reid (11)
Bedford High School, Leigh

Me

I am a sunflower,
I stand tall and see all.

I am Transylvania,
I am spooky and everyone knows me.

I am Gandalf,
Wise and know how to cope with problems.

I am the colour blue,
Not everyone likes me but I'm always there.

I am chocolate,
I can make people happy.

I am a wolf,
Silent and can get out of difficult situations.

Bradley Balmer (11)
Bedford High School, Leigh

I Am . . .

I am the colour yellow
Burning brightly inside . . .

I am the tiger cub
Lying in the blazing hot sun . . .

I am Blackpool Tower
Standing at my magnificent height
Beaming my decorative lights down
On the busy town . . .

I am a four-leaved clover
A gift of good luck whenever found . . .

I am a happy song
Easy to sing along to
Very lively and stays in your mind forever.

I am a bowl of ice
Cream, cool, sweet and delicious.

Emma Burke (11)
Bedford High School, Leigh

A Tranquil Soul

I am the colour orange
Playful, funny and cautious.

I am the countryside
Independent, quiet and obeying.

I am a panther,
Quiet, sneaky and stealthy,
Ready to pounce.

I am an oak tree,
Standing tall and offering shelter.

I am a jelly mousse,
Wobbling in the cool breeze.

Jake Barnes (12)
Bedford High School, Leigh

A Poem Of Me

I am the colour blue
Calm, tranquil and relaxed.

I am an energetic dolphin,
Jumping through the waves.

I am the rolling hills of Devon,
Wide open and serene.

I am a wild tulip,
Growing in the hills.

I am a cocoa bean,
Lots of things I can become.

I am a happy melody,
Sung in a celebratory crowd.

I am a lot of people,
But together they are me.

Craig Scott Gorman (11)
Bedford High School, Leigh

This Is Me

I am a bunny, hopping like a kangaroo
In a field of daisies,
I am a red rose in a colourful meadow,
I am a cat, sly like *Sylvester*,
I am a large sun, like the one in the sky,
I am a palm tree, peaceful and calm,
I am loving just like you.

Amy Louise Bell (12)
Bedford High School, Leigh

Metaphorical Me

I am maroon,
Calm and shrill in the breeze.

I'm a hungry monster,
Eating cheese.

I am an oak tree,
Graceful and tall.

I am Barbados,
Where there's no cares at all.

I am a squirrel,
Courteous and smug.

I am a worker ant,
The monarch's mug.

Brad Sewell (12)
Bedford High School, Leigh

The Open Window

The open window,
Through it all the leaves blowing,
Cold, square and small,
As white as snow,
As clear as dew drops on a petal,
It makes me freeze, just looking at it,
Like an ice block,
The open window,
Never go near the window,
You never know what will happen.

Helen Millington (11)
Bedford High School, Leigh

A Metaphorical Poem - I Am

I am the colour blue,
Lively, active but sometimes calm -
Like the sea at sunset.
I am a dolphin,
Wild, fast and intelligent,
Moving, racing with the wind.
I am the plant rape seed,
Bright, achieving lots when feeling free
But cut down by worry and fright.
I am the food chilli,
Fiery with answers and usually
Hot on top of work.
I am the song 'Trick Me',
Always jumpy and dancy, never being
Able to keep still - like a flag flying
During a gale.
I am the country America,
Busy, loud - always something
To do.
I am the character,
Mandy Hope,
Who is
Kind and good with
Animals
Although she can be moody.

Bethany Ward (11)
Bedford High School, Leigh

The Dog

The dog has four legs,
He sits down and begs,
He runs round on the floor
And barks when somebody is at the door
He's my big black fluffy mate,
Who is always chasing the postman at the gate.
My dog is called Pepe
I love him with all my heart
But when I am at school,
We are apart.

Natalie Wrigley (11)
Bedford High School, Leigh

The White Horse

The white horse,
Sometimes strong, sometimes weak,
White, soft and gentle,
As white as a ghost,
As soft as a kitten,
It makes me feel small,
Small as an ant,
White horse,
Riding it is the best.

Mia Evans (11)
Bedford High School, Leigh

The Tunnel

Trudging through the hollow dark tunnel,
I was in search of something bad,
The droning of the wind made it worse.

Taunted and
Fearful,
Haunted and
Tearful.

I could not go on,
I had to find it,
In the dark,
Or was this Hell?
I declared a stop,
And then I fell.

Death in a watery grave,
The tortured captives I could not save.

Liam O'Donnell (14)
Bedford High School, Leigh

One Cold Night

Clouded breath lingers in the cold air
Trees aglow in silvery light
Footsteps crunch on frozen crystals,
Moonbeams fill the starry night.

Glittering structures made of snow
Cast long shadows in the dark
Sprinkled with diamante star dust
Every bush radiates a spark.

Bitter cold biting at my ears and tail
My whiskers frozen like diamond thread
Bright eyes twinkle in the blackness
Tiny ice beads drop on my head.

Snowflakes falling, twisting, swirling
Silver dust covers the ground
Dazzling icicles all around
Paws pad quietly, don't make a sound.

Footprints trace the path I've taken
Through the park, across the town
Up the front steps, under the archway
To the flap of the house called home.

Yvonne Hodson (14)
Bedford High School, Leigh

This Lonely Day

The trees are swaying side to side,
On this windy and rainy day,
Nobody on the streets,
No children out to play.

She walks these streets alone,
Thoughts running through her mind.
Trying to think why, how,
Have her friends left her behind?

She wallows in her sadness,
Still nobody around.
Wondering why is she so alone?
Why can't she be found?

She shouldn't have to be alone,
Even on a day like this.
People should be there for her,
But they tend to have other business.

She starts to sob and make her sadness worse,
As though under some kind of dark curse.
The day seems to get longer as it goes on,
With no one to be there, no shoulder to lean on.

Knowing in her mind,
That she goes through this dilemma every day.
She tries to convince herself,
Never to be lonely again.

Danielle Lambert (14)
Bedford High School, Leigh

The Children

The perpetual droning of a watery scene,
Snow melting onto the floor taunting the ice-cold snow,
There was a tortured sound of a chilled breeze,
Which was matched only by the chanting of young children.

The young children having fun playing in the snow,
The melted ice forms a river that flows,
Flows through the drainpipes and into the streets,
And the road becomes nothing more than a water slide.

The icicles glittering as the cold sun shines,
And the clouds determined to crush the heat,
The cold that consumes the children,
Is challenged by the thick mittens they wear.

A heart-warming scene,
For everyone that passes by,
On this glorious winter's day,
It's a joy to your eye.

Robert Greenhalgh (14)
Bedford High School, Leigh

Autumn

Autumn
    falls
        across the land.
The morning brings
        a gloomy
            peace.

We bow our heads
        for summer's
            gone.

A mournful sorrow
        fills the air.
What will we do -
        now summer's
            gone?
And autumn feels it's here
        to stay.

Ben Eckersley (14)
Bedford High School, Leigh

An Insane Mind

Perpetual droning
Fails to deter
My black shadow creeping
Towards the wide-eyed innocent.

Silence is deafening
Among the glittering city
My tainted, blurred life
Is taunted by the will to die.

Their watery souls threatened
By my life alone
But they don't know
What it's like to hear the chanting.

No you don't know what it's like
When nothing feels all right
When you're lost
And alone.

When you're kicked when you're down
To be pushed around
To declare you're on the edge of breaking down
But no one's there to save you.

Welcome to my bitterly cold life.

Laura Owen (14)
Bedford High School, Leigh

Insomnia

Breathing laboured, body shaking,
I hide beneath the sheets,
For in the sanctuary of my bed,
I find some inner peace.

Lip trembling, eyelids prickling,
I dare to lift my head,
To find the shadows re-emerging,
My fear keeps their craving fed.

Face illuminated, fingers twitching,
In the none-existent breeze,
The bedroom curtain flutters for me,
I shift with most unease.

Hoisted upward, eyes now staring,
I think I hear some feet,
Beneath the door, a shadow slithers,
I hear the floorboards creak.

Clenched fists, face grimacing,
I scrutinise the room,
Rotating around me are shadows aplenty,
Dancing majestically in the gloom.

Sliding body, on the floor groping,
I crawl towards the light,
Hugging my knees, sat under my window,
'Will the moonlight save me tonight?'

Feeling thunderstruck, body swaying,
A thrashing object rattles my ribs,
Ascending upward through my throat,
'Am I really going to live?'

Disbelieving, own voice chanting,
I utter, 'This isn't real,'
Yet from behind me comes a tapping,
Yearning for a tasty meal.

Eyes prowling, I saw it coming,
Once again the floorboards creak,
A shower of light flares the room,
My tongue is in my cheek.

Voice hissing, illusions dissolving,
My mum stands at the door,
She turns the blazing bedroom light on,
And says, 'Not this once more!'

Footsteps shuffling, pointedly suggesting,
'Just turn on your TV,'
Shoves me in the bed, with one quick hug,
And there she let me be.

For my diary reaching, pen now scribbling,
I write the night's events neat,
For if they stay there, out of mind and sight,
I may just get some sleep . . .

Amy Evans (15)
Bedford High School, Leigh

Fallen Star

As the black sheet of night,
Wraps around me, rain hits the window,
Light reflects, all is bright,
But what happens when the lights go out?

As the black sheet closes in,
Nothing in silence can distract me,
The sky is lit by stars,
The stars fall faster and hit the ground.

As the black sheet fades,
We return from never waking up,
The sun takes over the sky,
And we wait for night and stars to fall.

Jodie Weatherley (14)
Bedford High School, Leigh

Winter Walk

Glittering lights shining
People as black shadows creeping
Traffic's perpetual droning
Eyes blurred and watery
Bitterly cold winds chill the air
Wide spaces seem so small
All seems threatening
Trees as though chanting
Taunting passers-by
Tortured by the cold
The declaration to myself
Makes me determined to return.

Nicola Costello (14)
Bedford High School, Leigh

Skating

Damp, watery coating,
Frozen by the chilled air,
Glittering in the sun.

Blades cutting through
The thick gleaming ice,
Skating gracefully on the long,
Wide ring,
Determined not to fall!

Perfect timing with the music,
Perfect, never missing a beat,
Perfect rhythm and posture.

Scores slowly appearing,
Crowds cheering and chanting,
Judges declaring - *perfect 10.*

Abigail Fish (14)
Bedford High School, Leigh

The Curse Of The Black Shadow

It all happened on the eighth of January, eighteen eighty five,
A mysterious fire was started by arson,
And Edward Dales was there and died,
The library after that was just a mound,
All the ancient reference books gone,
There was no evidence of who did this, found,
This is why there is a curse on Longseat High.

Every winter when it's chilly and cold,
The Black Shadow of Edward Dales creeps back,
To remind the children of what has taken place or so I'm told,
With watery black eyes and dressed in black,
Skulking round the buildings like a cat,
All he has with him is his trusty sack,
This is the Black Shadow.

Across the icy pond the wind groans,
The Black Shadow leaves footprints in the glittering snow,
As if Edward Dales himself moans,
Only the children see him,
Chanting, taunting in his perpetual droning voice.
For the teachers, all ideas of his existence have been thrown in the bin,
Not to be remembered, to be forgotten.

So that's the curse of The Black Shadow. Beware!
Beware of the ghost, he is very angry,
And the cupboard under the stairs is his lair,
So, never visit Longseat High in winter, or you will meet him.

Laura Sanders (14)
Bedford High School, Leigh

Winter's Coming

Winter's coming,
Dark draws nearer,
Snow falls, fires burn fiercely.

The sun goes down,
Dark has come , spiderwebs' crystals,
Winter's begun.

Christmas trees go up
On the 20th December,
Lights flashing,
Presents coming.

Chloé Anders (12)
Bedford High School, Leigh

Heaven And Hell

As the heavens shower down rain,
And the Devil's bathing in fire,
Is God watching our world fall apart,
And is this the Devil's desire?

As the Devil curses people with illness,
Does God make us better?
Does the Devil have a nice side?
Is it the same person altogether?

Or are they not a person?
Do they really exist?
Is Heaven all a lie?
Is the Bible desist?

Although, if this was all a story,
And none of it were true,
Why is there such religion?
Do you believe it too?

Daniel Hoffman (12)
Bedford High School, Leigh

My Brother Lewis!

I have a brother called Lewis,
He has dark blonde hair and blue eyes
I love him very much
And none of that is lies.

I will love him until the end
Even when he drives me round the bend
Most of the time we have fun together
And it will stay that way forever and ever.

Melissa Morris (13)
Bedford High School, Leigh

My Family

M any think they don't need a family,
Y ou're hopefully not one of them.

F amily are loving and sharing,
A nd they protect each other,
M ums and dads are caring,
I nside their home,
L oving, caring but not alone,
Y our family love you too.

Families are loving, caring
So give them some respect.

Robert Pickles (12)
Bedford High School, Leigh

The Top Sport

Football is the greatest sport,
Better than serving on a tennis court,
Scoring goals, saving shots,
That's why football is the tops.

Bolton Wanderers are my team,
Going for Europe is our dream,
Scoring goals, saving shots,
That's why football is the tops.

In my spare time I like to play cricket,
But I'd rather watch Bolton with my season ticket,
Scoring goals, saving shots,
That's why football is the tops.

Martin Pendlebury (12)
Bedford High School, Leigh

Welcome To My World

Welcome to my world,
My world of,
Love, peace and joy,
In my life,
People have come and gone,
As I grow older, I become wiser,
This is my world.

In my life,
I have seen,
Winter, the cold, icy month,
Spring, the month where
Little lambs are born,
Summer the hottest month,
And autumn, the times
When leaves fall,
This is my world,
The one and only world.

Rebecca Naughton (12)
Bedford High School, Leigh

Snowball

Frozen branches creak,
As children seek for the perfect snowball,
Down by the frozen frosty creek,
The children seek the perfect snowman,
They had a plan but all fails
When they try to sail the boat
On the frozen creek.

Adam Nutsey (12)
Bedford High School, Leigh

Winter's Coming

Winter's coming with ice-cold snow,
Where did spring and summer go?
Building snowmen, having fights,
Coughs and colds with frostbite.

Trees are covered with pure white,
The grass also becomes white,
The snowflakes glisten at night,
Especially in moonlight.

The streets are getting darker,
The street lamps act as a marker,
The snow is slowly melting,
As the hail is hardly pelting.

Then it starts pelting,
The hail starts melting,
The snow starts fading,
As the morning starts breaking.

Shauna Amber Rushworth (13)
Bedford High School, Leigh

Big Shake

Big shake, small Earth,
Danger chases us,
Houses falling, people shout,
Animals running,
Where to go?
Houses disappearing, one after another,
Smoke surrounding,
Why do we have to suffer?

Jamie Hughes (12)
Bedford High School, Leigh

Why Did You Have To Go?
(In loving memory of my grandad)

I'm walking slowly as a cloud when tears come to my eyes,
Even when I'm happy,
Inside I feel sad,
Why did you have to go?

The world feels so big without you here,
A part of me is missing,
I miss you here by my side,
I wish you were here to help me,
Why did you have to go?

Don't forget I think of you,
You're always on my mind,
I look up to you,
And I miss you,
Why did you have to go?

I'm walking slowly as a cloud when tears come to my eyes,
Even when I'm happy,
Inside I feel sad,
Why did you have to go?

Katie Hilton (13)
Bedford High School, Leigh

Friends

Friends are good,
Best friends are the best,
They are there when you're down,
They will always be around,
They are a shoulder to cry on,
A person to rely on,
You'll have a lot of good times,
But sometimes there'll be bad times,
A good time running through the park,
Or playing murderer in the dark,
Playing hide-and-seek,
Make sure you don't peek,
Having a great big sleepover,
All your mates will stop over,
Stuffing your face with pizza,
Talking about a girl called Lisa,
Watching loads of scary films,
And doing a great deal of other things,
Friends are good, very rarely bad,
But best of friends beat the rest.

Lee Johnson (12)
Bedford High School, Leigh

A Metaphorical Me

I am the colours purple and lilac,
Bold, but sometimes shy.

I am a cheetah,
Always on the move, fast across the jungle floor.

I am the city New York,
Full of hustle and bustle, loud and bright.

I am a dandelion,
Wild and outgoing.

I am a pizza,
With as many moods as toppings.

I am the song 'Come With Me' by Special D,
Fun, lively and jumpy.

I am the character 'Courtney' from 'Bring It On'
Loud, moody and cocky.

Alyesha Sayle (11)
Bedford High School, Leigh

All About Me

I am the colour yellow
Blazed jewels in the sky.

I am a cheetah,
Fast, furious and quick off the mark.

I am a sunflower,
Who brightens everybody's day and makes the night
Seem so far away.

I am a red-hot chilli pepper,
Fiery, spicy and ready for action.

I am Disneyland,
Full of life and colourful.

I am the song 'Life is a Roller Coaster' by Ronan Keating,
I'm either up or down, or going round and round.

Rebecca Pyke (11)
Bedford High School, Leigh

A Metaphorical Me

I am the colour yellow,
Like the sun shining over the world.

I am a cheetah,
Running across the plains of Africa.

I am London's town centre,
Full of energetic people rushing
In and out of shops.

I am a daisy,
Small, wild but strong.

I am a bowl of noodles,
As small, thin and moving all over the place.

I am the song 'Fighter'
Fast, loud and I stick up for myself.

I am the character 'Star',
Noisy and scared of no one.

Laura Atherton (11)
Bedford High School, Leigh

A Metaphorical Poem About
Philippa Louise Heath

I am the colour red,
Quick off the mark, fiery and mad.

I am the animal, tortoise,
I walk at my own pace.

I am the town Southport,
Improving all the time.

I am a sunflower,
I love the sizzling warm sun.

I am the song,
'All Things Bright and Beautiful.'

I am the character,
'Winnie the Pooh', sweet and loveable.

Philippa Heath (11)
Bedford High School, Leigh

This Is Me!

I am red because it can be lively but also dull!
I am a fox, I am very sly and cunning!
I am Las Vegas because it is very lively!
I am French Lavender because it can be nice
                    But also not very nice!
I am pizza or potatoes because I can be a variety
                    of different things!
I am 'Come With Me' because it's lively and I
                    always make people have fun,
I am Harry Potter, I am adventurous!

Daniel Haydock (11)
Bedford High School, Leigh

Poetry

Poetry is like a rose,
Poetry is like water that flows like a river,
Poetry is art.

Anger, joy, love, hope,
Emotions are poetry,
Nonsense, good, evil, envy,
Anything can be made into poetry.

Poetry is a gift,
It is a gift of expression,
It can be used to say,
Congratulations, Happy Birthday or even Farewell.

Stanza, simile, metaphors,
Rhythm, rhyme,
All used in poetry.

So poetry is everywhere,
Inspiration is everywhere,
In the Earth, in the sky,
Even in the great big universe.

So you see poetry is art.

Samanta Chan (12)
Bedford High School, Leigh

Money

Money is greed, laughter and gain,
Money is food, suffering and pain,
Money for the rich,
None for the poor,
Whoever we are, we still want more.

Sam Hughes (13)
Bedford High School, Leigh

All About Me

I am orange,
Bright, sunny and warm.

I am a fox,
Fast, sly and alert.

I am the Arctic,
Cold, shivering and icy.

I am a rose,
Sharp, colourful and scented.

I am a pizza,
Tasty, crusty and cheesy.

I am the song 'Happy Birthday'
Glad, cheerful and celebrate.

I am 'Klaus' from 'A Series of Unfortunate Events,'
Because he is smart, cunning and a good reader.

Isaac Southern (11)
Bedford High School, Leigh

All About Me

I am orange,
Happy and as bright as the sun.

I am a monkey,
Cheeky and a good tree climber.

I am Anglesey in Wales,
Sunny and hot.

I'm a sunflower,
Tall and bright.

I'm a banana,
Tall and colourful.

'Making Your Mind Up'
I can never make up my mind.

I am 'Shrek'
Tall and funny.

Martin Slater (11)
Bedford High School, Leigh

Me

I am light blue,
Calm and bright.

I am a bear,
Tall and fierce.

I am Majorca,
Bright and calm.

I am a sunflower,
Tall and bright.

I am a pie,
Large and crunchy.

I am 'Come With Me'
Nice and fast.

I am 'Dom'
Loud and annoying.

Jack Ryan (11)
Bedford High School, Leigh

Me In A Poem

I am the colour red, fiery and wanting
To burn ground quickly.

I am New York City, bright and colourful,
Like the lights at night.

I am a cheetah, I don't like waiting and
I want to get things over and done with.

I am Tracy Beaker, daring and inventive,
I am 'Come With,' nice and fast.

Michael Ashton (11)
Bedford High School, Leigh

A Metaphorical Me

I am the colour orange,
Like a Jaffa ready to burst!
I am a horse,
Elegant but wild.
I am Spain,
Wild with the nightlife, but
Calm with the views.
I am a sunflower,
Tall, sunny but attract fiery wasps.
I am a strawberry, sweet, bright
But some people think I'm sour.
I am the tune 'Vogue',
Slow, but then fast,
I am Cinderella,
I work on a farm,
But I have a glamorous life too.

Hannah Sloan (11)
Bedford High School, Leigh

This Is Me

I am the midnight, sea-blue sky,
My starry eyes watch over you,
I am the vibrant morning sun,
Laughing, smiling, full of fun,
I am a little wallaby,
I will cheer you up,
I am the summertime breezy winds,
That calm you down when tempers flare,
I am the beach,
You can relax with me,
All cares float away.

Amanda Young (11)
Bedford High School, Leigh

I Am . . .

I am the colour of red,
Fiery but cheerful and mad.

I am a tiger,
Wild, crazy but soft.

I am the town of Ibiza,
Non-stop, lively and outgoing.

I am an orchid,
Expensive with a range of qualities.

I am 'Babycakes'
Mad, wild and hyper.

I am 'Drew Barrymore'
Hair, colour, attitude and style.

Rebecca Ward (11)
Bedford High School, Leigh

At The Fair

Oh what a fantastic experience this is, can you hear me?
I'm sorry, we can only just hear you, there is a strong interference.
You wouldn't believe what I am experiencing right now . . .

The creatures of this planet are . . .

Pieces of matter stuck in a spinning counter,
Sounds emptying in the atmosphere,
Colours whirling and twirling around them,
Some have pink fluffy clouds stuck to their faces.

They are stabbing yellow objects with bits of fluff
                                        attached to their heads.
In exchange for wobbly jelly with a triangle at the end
                                        that swirls in liquid,
And fluffballs stuck together like one of us.

They have captured a long spaceship and fastened
It to a track with pieces of matter snared inside.
Big ones and small ones, round ones and short ones,
Drift under an orange ball.

Emma Haworth (13)
Booth Hall Hospital School, Manchester

Broken Child

As I awake from a dream
An image of a child forms in the corner of my room
She's cold, distant
Her icy stare into the unknown
Tells the world she's broken.

As she lays in the shadows of my room
I begin to see her features
A beautiful darkness surrounds her
Dark brown locks spiral down over her face like a waterfall
Her eyes are dark, full of anger, pain and sadness.

Her icy glare melts into a broken child's tearful plea
With four words, my heart breaks at such a simple request
That I cannot grant
'I wanna go home,' she begs me before she once again
Drifts into the unknown.

As she slowly rises in an effort to embrace me
I hear her plea resounding in my head
Suddenly, the temperature lowers
Her embrace is chilling; she dissolves in me.

I hear her echo, 'I wanna go home.'
As I lay down in the shadowed corner of my room
I sadly whisper, 'Me too.'

Alexandra Kate Bagust (15)
Falinge Park High School, Rochdale

That Night

One night under my bed,
I heard a voice and it said,
'Give me your money,
Give me your life,
Or it will end in the
Swipe of a knife.'
At first I thought it was a dream,
Then I started to sweat
And started to scream,
I thought this was the night
That I would die,
I looked under my bed
And started to cry,
Then my mum came in and
Said 'Time for school,'
I realised it was a dream
And felt such a fool.

Emma Jones & Kim Watson (13)
Hope High School, Salford

Playtime Ghost

She stood looking at me in the mirror,
Maybe she thought that I was her killer,
I wanted to run, I had fear for my life,
As she went in her pocket and pulled out a knife,
I stood there frozen, only to see,
That the girl was talking right back at me,
A little blue tear rolled down her eye,
So I asked, 'Oh little girl why do you cry?'
She put her hand on her heart and quietly said,
'I will now tell you the reason why I am dead,
They punched me and kicked me and threw me against the door,
They hurt me and bruised me until I lay motionless on the floor,
Here I am stuck in this mirror,
All because of my playtime *killer!*'

Chantelle Archer & Abigail Wilde (13)
Hope High School, Salford

Miller's End

I was out at night alone without a friend,
When I found myself at Miller's End.

I looked behind, no footprints could I trace,
I seem to have been drawn to this place,

I felt as if my feet were being dragged across the floor,
As they slowly led me to the door,

I saw a face at the windowpane,
Which waved at me again and again,

With trembling fingers I pressed the bell,
Which opened the door to the gates of Hell . . .

Leonie Marsh (13)
Hope High School, Salford

Alone There

As I walked down the street,
A ghostly lady I did meet,
She seemed as if she was afloat,
As she walked way with her flowing coat.
The trees whistled, growled and shook,
But there I stood all I could do was look.
All of a sudden, she vanished into thin air,
Alone I stood, alone stood there.

Katie Sargeson (13)
Hope High School, Salford

My Little Brother

He's got blond hair and bright blue eyes
He's very cheeky and tells porky pies,
He likes to play out and has good fun,
He likes football, cricket and enjoys to run.
He likes watching wrestling and playing with toys,
He certainly does make a lot of noise,
He likes to play out with his brother's mates,
He has to stay in, that's what he hates,
I'll always love my little bruv
No matter what he does,
He sometimes gets his own way,
But I will still always play,
That's the end about my brother,
And that's why I couldn't choose any other.

Ashleigh Vennard (13)
Hope High School, Salford

Rain, Rain, Rain

The rain, rain, rain,
It races down the windowpane,
Water everywhere,
But no one seems to care.
Rain, rain, rain,
It can cause floods,
So when it's about, people put up their hoods,
It can be fine, it can be heavy,
It bounces up and down on the red cherry,
Rain! Rain! Rain!

Alex Tomlinson (13)
Hope High School, Salford

Ghost At The Door

A big bad billionaire purchased the town of
Sleepy Hollow,
Built it how he wished,
But he never knew the secret of the town,
People rolled the money in and he never cared,
Said a speech and got off.

Everyone partied into the night,
They never knew the secret,
The town hall clock rang twelve,
Trees rustled,
The autumn leaves swirled and swayed,
At the entrance to the town,
A ghostly figure appeared,
When he laughed it was sheer evil.

He entered the town, everyone panicked,
He jumped off his horse,
Drew two blades,
He charged in force
And chopped everyone like sardines,
Sleepy Hollow was no more!

Thomas Lane (13)
Hope High School, Salford

The Lost Boys

There was a big, dark and damp ship,
Where the sea was rough and loud,
There were two lost boys in the cabin,
They were dressed as tramps with no shoes.

The boys were twelve and thirteen years old,
They were called John and Peter,
On the ship there was a big bang,
The floors were creaking and rattling.

There were loud noises on the ship,
The boys were getting scared and started to cry,
There was a bang on the door and Peter opened it,
There was nobody there and then John shut the door.

The people on the ship were scaring the boys,
They were dressed up and they were Peter and John's mates really,
And they just tried to scare them because,
The day was 31st October 1998.

Steven White (13)
Hope High School, Salford

Forest

Near my house there was a forest,
Dark and tall its trees,
No one dared to enter except the simple honeybees.

But that was all about to change,
Following the events of something strange.
It was what everybody feared,
A little boy had disappeared,
Everyone looked high and low,
But after many days they still had nothing to show.
For they still hadn't ventured into the forest.

But soon it could be held off no more
For a child's cry could be heard from within.
So off they went in search of the bone-chilling din.
But day after day the search parties went in,
Returning with less and less hope.

Many years have passed,
And still the search is on,
For the distant cries still call out,
Call out for help.

Elizabeth Trousdale (13)
Hope High School, Salford

I Saw A Ghost!

Under my bed,
In my room,
In the middle of the night,
It was very scary,
My mum didn't believe me,
My dad said I was dreamin'
Even though I was screamin'.

One night not long after this,
I heard my mum screamin'
She didn't say why,
My dad was scared
But I was laughing.
I didn't believe them,
All because they told me ghosts weren't real!

I carried on laughing all through the night,
I couldn't see how they were scared,
Because when I was screamin' they never cared.

My mum and dad really care,
All because they got a scare!

Letitia Bumby & Nichola Johnson (13)
Hope High School, Salford

The Headless Horseman

One scary night, on Hallowe'en,
In an empty graveyard, no one to be seen.
There wasn't a sound to be heard,
Not even the chirp of a passing bird.
Then suddenly, from behind a headstone,
Something or someone made a loud groan.
My heart started beating triple time,
With a million things racing through my mind.
Was it a ghost, witch or ghoul,
Or maybe just me being a fool?
I started walking quicker than before,
I could hear my feet beating on the floor.
As I turned a corner, round the graves,
I heard a gallop and a couple of neighs.
I sharply turned and started to stare,
Wondering and asking who was there.
Then from a distance I started to see,
An animal of some sort running to me.
It looked like a horse with a mysterious rider,
And had eight legs just like a spider,
As it came closer, nearer to me,
It was then that I started to see,
Instead of a head on his shoulders,
Was a pumpkin as round as a boulder!
Infested with bugs, maggots and worms,
I could feel, inside, my stomach turn.

Samantha Ledwith (13)
Hope High School, Salford

The Darkness

There is a place in the darkness,
where no kid would ever go,
but this brave lad was very brave,
he went into the darkness,
and he disappeared into darkness.

He walked and walked, he never stopped,
he never fell, he never coughed,
he saw trees and trees and never stopped,
he always knew it wouldn't stop,
but he couldn't stop because it was like a jungle.

He saw a light, could it be
the house where no kid could ever go,
he ran and ran and never stopped,
he stumbled and tumbled and fell
he woke up in a room like a death room.

Blood! Blood across the room,
he was scared, he was tough,
but could he escape or could he not?
He saw a knife, he saw some chance,
he cut and cut and cut it off.

He walked over, very scared,
he saw the body over by the ceiling,
he noticed the body,
it was his dad, very still, could it be a ceiling killer.
He left the scary room . . .

He went down the stairs,
he saw a flare,
he saw his killer,
this was a chiller,
his killer had a saw.

He ran down and down the stairs,
the killer chopped his legs,
then he sliced hard while he screamed,
in the forest dark at night.
You can still hear the screams now.

And that was a scary thriller.

Dale Evans (13)
Hope High School, Salford

Dark Alleys

In the night
alleys are scary,
you expect to turn round
and see something hairy.
You either creep about
or run very fast,
don't care what it is
as long as it's passed.

Matthew Rothwell (13)
Hope High School, Salford

Brave Dave

There was a man called Dave
Who thought he was brave,
He went up a hill
And he saw a cave.
He went in there
And it was very dark.
It was full of animals like Noah's Ark,
He said, 'This is not scary,'
A big bear jumped out,
Then he ran like a fairy!

Andrew Ditchett (13)
Hope High School, Salford

Ghost Dream

Phoebe had a dream
Which came true,
She heard a loud scream,
As the ghost came through.

Lydia took baby to bed,
While Phoebe made a drink,
Phoebe thought she was dead,
So Phoebe had to think.

Parents weren't back till two,
Baby was crying all night,
Phoebe didn't know what to do,
Worrying, was baby alright?

Lydia came back with a fright,
Then tried to used the phone,
While Phoebe held baby tight,
But it wouldn't work so they were all alone.

Knock, knock, on the door,
Rattle, rattle, oh my God,
It was the ghost coming through the floor,
Cry, cry, 'Help me PC Plodd.'

She wrapped her hands around my neck,
Phoebe awoke and didn't know what to do.
Lydia was a wreck.
Dreams do come true!

Paige Wilson & Leanne Davenport (13)
Hope High School, Salford

Murder

The blade glinted in the light
On a very dark night.
The eyes were bright
Which gave the victim a fright.
The murderer smiled a rare smile,
The assigned victim was called Kyle.
The victim screamed
As the knife gleamed.
The murderer attacked
With terrible impact.
The hit was done,
To the murderer it was fun.

Alex King (13)
Hope High School, Salford

My Nana

My nana always says to me,
'What have you got there . . .
Jonathon,
James,
Joe,
Barbara,
John,
Sam,
Linda,
Hannah,
Paul!'

Paul Derbyshire (12)
Hope High School, Salford

The Lazy Dog

The lazy dog,
Does he move?
Does he play?
No, he sleeps all day!

Does he have a wash?
Does he groom his hair?
Does he chew his nails?
No, he sleeps all day!

Does he bark?
Does he beg?
Does he cry?
No, he sleeps all day!

Does he have a drink?
Does he have a laugh?
Does he eat?
No, he sleeps all day!

Jemma Craven (13)
Hope High School, Salford

The Big Match

I am so excited
Because it's City vs United.

The journey there is quite a fright,
But I can't wait for tonight.

As the referee starts the game,
The players know this game's not going to be the same.

The first goal goes in like a bullet through a tin,
The other team's chances of winning are very, very thin.

The second goal goes in,
It is scored by a Finn.

Now we're 2-0 up,
And we've definitely won the cup.

Jonathan Stanley (13)
Hope High School, Salford

The Wind

I am a wolf, ferocious and howling,
I am a dog, barking and growling,
I am a breeze to keep them cool,
I am a child dancing like a fool,
I am a force blowing them about,
I am a person loving just to shout, shout, shout!

Sara Fishwick (14)
Hope High School, Salford

Hallowe'en

The pumpkins are lit up,
the children are collecting sweets in a cup.

The ghosts come to give you a fright,
on this special night.

It's dark and scary,
and costumes and masks are hairy.

Tonight's the night for the evil queen,
because tonight it's Hallowe'en.

Rachael Conway (13)
Hope High School, Salford

The Fish's Luck!

Up they scoop me and away I go,
Everything around me seems to be moving slow.
I was just swimming within the reeds,
If only I hadn't been full of greed.

I see the glistening hook,
I just have to take a look,
I bite the bait,
I've just sealed my fate.

The pain is too much to bear
And I'm gasping for air.
It's all going black
As the fisherman puts me in his sack.

Hannah Taylor (13)
Hope High School, Salford

Getting Ready For School

I get up in the morning
although I'm still yawning,
then I go downstairs
without any cares.
I can't find my tie,
and I don't know why.
My mum looks and then asks,
I know, my room, my daily tasks.
I run upstairs and trip over a shoe
and find my homework which is due.
I'm already late.
It's a cruel fate,
the bus comes on time
but I'm back of the line.
I get to school
but I must be a fool.

Zoey Hyland (13)
Hope High School, Salford

Home Alone

Everyone has gone on holiday,
But I've been left at home,
All alone.

I wander round the house,
You could hear the squeak of a mouse,
It's all so very quiet,
When normally my house is like living in the middle of a riot.

I can't find anything to eat,
Not even a slice of meat.

Hopefully my family will be back soon,
Before the rise of the next moon.

Adam Mitchell (13)
Hope High School, Salford

The Man In The Moon

The man in the moon
came down to soon
to see the Earth
which gave birth
to all the trees, the birds and bees.

He visited Mars,
saw many stars
but not any people
and not any cars.

Next journey was Pluto
where living things don't grow
very icy and cold
very rock I'm told.

He ventured next to the sun
didn't see anyone
needed sunglass though
very hot and no snow!

Back to the moon
the little man zoomed
to tell of his find
to all mankind!

Next trip's in December
do hope he'll remember
to keep us in mind
maybe take me with him next time.

Brooke Lever (12)
Hope High School, Salford

The Disaster Queen

She is the queen of disaster,
What she hasn't done I wouldn't ask her,
From cracking the pots
To breaking the locks,
From spilling the beans
To ripping someone's jeans,
She is the disaster queen!

Help! Help! Don't send the queen,
I do not want her on this disaster scene,
She always means well,
It's not her fault people rebel,
Why can we not see her goodness?
Well that's easy, because all we see is her clumsiness.

Danielle Howcroft (12)
Hope High School, Salford

Untitled

I have a puppy called Max,
He plays all day with the ball.
He likes to bite your socks
As he runs up and down the hall.
He's only very small but he barks like he's very tall.

Elliott Collins (13)
Hope High School, Salford

The Mighty Hero

It was 0-0 just after half-time,
He shot from the halfway line,
He was bored
Now he'd scored
With his left foot
Only because he's Dutch.
Now he celebrated
Not getting relegated,
The mighty hero.

Then he shot again,
Denied by the keeper's save,
Not all that bad,
The other team were all good lads,
A mighty hero.

He scored a penalty,
It was his second goal,
His celebration was a role,
He was really in control,
The mighty hero.

The final whistle blew,
He was shaking hands with number 2,
Now we'd won,
The terrace shouted, 'Well done!'
Who was I?
The mighty hero!

Robert Carroll (12)
Hope High School, Salford

Rolley The Hamster

He rolls round
the room, laughing
to himself. Running
in his ball till he has
found his place.

Into the next room
he goes *bang* and *boom*
as he enters the
other room rolling,
then eats his food.

Crash, bang, smash,
in the kitchen,
banging to the cooker
and even crashing
to the fridge and
don't forget the door!

Now he's found
his place again,
nice and quiet,
finally lots of peace!

Danielle Davies (12)
Hope High School, Salford

My School Life

When I was five
I felt so alive,
Nursery was great,
I was never late
Else I would miss all the fun,
Carrying the boxes which weighed a ton.

Then I moved on,
It was like life'd been a con,
From carrying boxes which weighed a ton
To having no fun.
It was all homework and playtime shortened down,
I even had marks where I'd begun to frown.

Then it got better, I was now in secondary school,
There was still not a lot of fun, no playing in the pool,
But I met new friends, the coolest thing to me,
Then I realised school is the best place you can ever be!

Alissa Holloway (12)
Hope High School, Salford

Changes

Everything changes
we can't
stop it.

You will change,
you may get taller,
you may get smarter,
but you will change.

Everything changes
we can't
stop it!

When you change
you may not like what you've become,
but everything changes,
nothing may have changed yet,
but everything changes

And
we can't stop
it!

Joshua Blakeley (12)
Hope High School, Salford

Hallowe'en

H allowe'en is mint,
A day to have fun,
L oud and happy,
L aughing and joking,
O ur friends trick or treating with us,
W e have lots of fun all night,
E xcited and can't wait,
E xplode with joy,
N ew costumes.

Lucinda Corbelle (13)
Hope High School, Salford

Puppy Ben

I have a puppy called Ben,
he likes to chew our things,
the phone wire and the toilet roll, and
he barks when the doorbell rings!

Dean Pinkney (12)
Hope High School, Salford

Face

Look at my face,
It is such a disgrace,
There are blisters and bruises, bumps and cuts,
It feels like my life has gone completely nuts!

I am so ashamed,
But I am the one to blame,
I jumped in that car,
And I went too far!

My mum always told me not to talk to a stranger,
But I ignored her rule and put myself in danger.
I could have been alright and walked off with my friend,
But I went without knowing it could be the end.

I can't believe I was such a fool,
Accepting a lift was so uncool,
All of my face was tender and swollen,
I should have know that my ride was
Stolen!

Gemma Cheyne (13)
Kirkham Grammar School, Preston

All Alone

All alone
No one's home,
The faint drip of a tap that no one fixed,
He can see you're alone in your home.

Walking along the street,
And you get that
Feeling on the back of your neck
That someone is watching you.

Some funny shapes,
A clown with a knife,
Creatures crawling around,
Get on the floor, stay right down.

The branches lashing out
Like an angry person
Trying to grab you,
A tormenting figure.

Something is lingering in the shadows.

Bethany Walsh (12)
Kirkham Grammar School, Preston

My First Day

I got up in the morning, I was really excited,
I saw my uniform, I was so delighted.
When I was dressed, my photo was taken,
I just had time for some eggs and bacon.

When I set off to catch the bus,
My mum and dad made a big fuss.
I made some friends on the way to school,
They were really funny, silly and cool.

When I arrived, I went to the hall,
I was so nervous and felt so small,
I met my teachers, they were really kind,
They gave me a diary which had to be signed.

Dinner was nice, I had chilli and rice,
The doughnuts were yummy but bad for your tummy.
I went outside to see my friends,
It seemed like lunchtime would never end.

I had French and drama in the afternoon,
I was having fun but it was home time soon.
It was a long and happy day for us all,
And now I don't feel so small.

My first day at Kirkham was really fab,
I can't wait for the new biology lab.
So thanks a lot for a brilliant day,
And wish me luck on my way.

Hannah Gardner (11)
Kirkham Grammar School, Preston

Face = Disgrace

My face
Is my disgrace;
I look in the mirror and see
A stranger staring back at me;
If I had not been so lame,
I would still be the same.
I should have stayed away from fire,
And not stuck around with a liar.
I took that dare,
Like I didn't care,
But when I got stuck,
I thought I'd run out of luck.
When the flames started to lick;
I felt I was incredibly thick.
It was my lucky day,
Yet I didn't get completely away.
The flames took my identity,
And now to strangers I'm an oddity.
My face
Is my disgrace!

Leonora Gaskell (13)
Kirkham Grammar School, Preston

What Happened?

I look at my face and all I remember,
Is the terrible accident
On the 10th of November.

The flashbacks are here,
Hold tight, do not fear,
The worst part has passed
When I was going too fast.

Down country lanes,
In a car of my own,
Anastacia is singing
In a wonderful tone.

Nor paying attention
To the wet, icy roads,
'Everything is fine,'
But really, who knows?

The wheels start to swerve,
I worry, I panic,
Whatever should I do?
I thought this car was new!

But the car it was not,
The driver it was,
And before I knew it,
I think I was hit.

I get to the hospital,
They treat my injuries with care.
I want to look at my face,
But really, do I dare?

My injuries are horrific and I'm totally deformed,
My face, I just can't stand it,
A plastic surgeon should be informed.

Claire Pasquill (14)
Kirkham Grammar School, Preston

Car Crash

Ooh my face,
It hurts so much.
I'm burnt all over,
It's too sore to touch.

I'm frightened,
I don't understand,
I'm so confused,
Will someone give me a helping hand?

I look so different,
My face is swollen,
What's happening to me?
It's like a curse that will never be broken.

What should I do?
What should I say?
I'm going to look like this,
Day after day.

How many grafts
Will it take
To put this face back into shape?

Camille Knowles (13)
Kirkham Grammar School, Preston

A Scary World

Owls hooting,
Demons tormenting,
Robbers shooting,
Witches lurking.

Lost spirits creeping,
Kittens wailing,
Mice sleeping,
Green eyes searching.

Creatures stalking,
Ghost hunting,
Me walking,
People grunting.

Mongrels asleep,
I'm still alone,
I can't speak,
I want to go home.

I wake up suddenly,
I look around,
I start shuddering,
It's a scary world.

Rebecca Lewis (12)
Kirkham Grammar School, Preston

Fear

As I walk home
The trees twist and creak,
Vicious hands clawing at me.

As I walk home
Cats howl and scream,
Turning my blood to ice.

As I walk home
Shadows flicker and fade,
Stalking me.

As I walk home
It all seems scary
Considering it's only 3.30!

John Platt (12)
Kirkham Grammar School, Preston

The Forest

Some rustling leaves,
A whispering whimper,
A hooting owl,
Echoing from the trees.

A howling gale,
Voices on the wind,
Misshapen faces
Amongst the sinister trees.

Spirits drifting,
Highwaymen crouching,
A net of ants
Rampaging along.

A shadowy outline
Lingering in the shadows,
Creeping along,
Ready to kill.

Grace Ford (12)
Kirkham Grammar School, Preston

Hurricane Alley

The squeals of it,
The howling of it,
The fear of it,
It's Hurricane Alley.

The rampaging of it,
The speed of it,
The strength of it,
It's fearful Hurricane Alley.

The nightmare of it,
The fright of it,
The evil of it,
It's nasty Hurricane Alley.

The power of it,
The destruction of it,
The damage of it,
It's strong Hurricane Alley.

Sam Greensmith (12)
Kirkham Grammar School, Preston

The Dream Fight

I'm twelve years old,
but one of the best boxers in the world.
Tonight was the fight of my life,
against Muhammad Ali.
It was a desperate fight,
but I had the advantage.
I kept dodging,
but he kept coming back.
He packed powerful punches,
but so did I.
I was small,
so hard to hit.
After a desperate fight,
I hit him one last time.
So that night I won,
only twelve years old.
I loved that night,
the night I won the Championship fight.

Ryan Hutchings (12)
Kirkham Grammar School, Preston

My Worst Nightmare!

Rustling, crunching, stomping feet,
Centre of the woods is where they meet,
Throwing, hitting, screaming on the floor,
Ripping, slicing, screeching no more.
All I could see was a mis-shapen face.
It made me cold and hesitant,
He took out a huge, silver knife,
She let out a cry,
It was the end of her life!

Danielle Simpson (12)
Kirkham Grammar School, Preston

A Disturbing Dream

A shadowy figure,
Rustling leaves,
A creaking house,
Alone in the dark,
A power cut.

Flickering candles,
Shadows cast on walls,
A flash of lightning,
A distant rumble,
A door creaks open.

A sudden draught,
Crunching gravel outside,
No one comes,
Whistling wind,
An owl hoots.

A full moon,
Clouds skittering across the sky,
Something howls
As the lights flicker on and off,
A woman appears . . .

Grace O'Flaherty (12)
Kirkham Grammar School, Preston

A Moment Of Fear

Deserted, black night,
crunching leaves,
whistling wind,
a shadowy outline
coming closer and closer.

Striking lightning,
running, stumbling,
going faster and faster,
alone in the dark.

A full moon,
mis-shapen shapes everywhere;
I shut my eyes tight,
screaming, screeching,
gone, into a world of darkness;
I slowly open my eyes
and it was a nightmare!

Francesca Hughes (12)
Kirkham Grammar School, Preston

A Lesson Learnt

What has happened to my face?
I think that it is a disgrace,
It looks to me that it is disfigured,
The look that would not be mirrored.

The accident nearly killed me,
We turned a corner and hit a tree,
The car was going very fast,
The present, no future, a past.

My friends and family waiting there,
Quiet thoughts they all did share,
Sat in silence, not a word,
Bad news was all they heard.

The mask I wear is no longer me,
A sorry sight for all to see,
Red and crinkled, shrivelled and burnt,
There is a lesson that has now been learnt.

Andrew Bayliss (13)
Kirkham Grammar School, Preston

Burnt

I jumped into the car
With no fear at all.
What is there to worry
I know them all.

I didn't fasten my seat belt,
And with a screech, off we went,
Onto the kerb and down the road, which I regret!
As we flew, the faster we got.

With a bang I came to a sudden stop!
We rolled over and over and around and around,
I came to a stop as I hit the ground,
There was no light, there was no sound, I lay there burning
As my heart began to pound.

I woke the next day, I looked all around,
'What is this place?' I wanted to cry aloud,
I tried and tried but I could not hear,
No sound or movement, just a tear

On my cheek, burning its way down,
Then *plop* as it hit the ground,
Why is my cheek so hot? I thought.
Not flexing, not stretching the way it ought,
As I lay there motionless, sleeping on the hard, smashed-up car.

When I woke up, to my right,
A man with a stretcher, what a sight!
And with a swish, to my delight,
I was lifted up and out of sight.

Simon Brooker (14)
Kirkham Grammar School, Preston

A Mistake

Why me? Why my face?
There are bumps and lumps all over the place!
It's so uneven all around, everyone's looking,
No expression, no sound.

I wish I hadn't been so dumb!
'Don't be crazy!' I was told by some,
All I remember is the car going round,
Dizzy sensation, lots of sound.

I wonder what happened to the rest.
Am I in denial if it happens to the best?
I wonder if they were ever found.
Confused expressions, a thinking sound.

What will people think of me?
They'll look at me, a monster they'll see,
They'll hate me, my sorrows are drowned,
Scared expression, in my head the sound.

Chris Monaghan (13)
Kirkham Grammar School, Preston

My Facelift

My face, it's gone!
That's it, I'm over and done!
Why me? What did I do?
It's not fair, I was the same as you.

Before I was handsome and had lots of friends,
But now I am ugly, my face, uneven ends.
I'm so angry, why did I get in the car?
If I hadn't my face wouldn't look like tar.

Bumps, bruises, cuts all over the place,
To me, I am such a disgrace!
Why did I get in the car? I should have given it a miss,
But I didn't . . . and now . . . I look like this.

Jordan Ledger (13)
Kirkham Grammar School, Preston

Why Me?

Life isn't the same now,
People staring,
People asking,
People judging.

I look in the mirror each morning,
Not to see me, my beautiful face,
But someone else,
A mutant, Frankenstein face.

It isn't well laid-out and soft-skinned,
It is scarred, disfigured,
Not me,
Full of frightening memories and past worries.

I should never have got into that car
With that reckless driver,
With his cigarette that set the car alight,
That burned my face off.

I daren't go out in the day,
I have lost all my friends,
I can't take it anymore!
Why? Why me?

Maria Hindley (13)
Kirkham Grammar School, Preston

Crash

How did this happen?
Why to me?
Bruised and burnt,
How can this be?

How did this happen?
Was it me?
Was it a crash?
I just can't see!

How did this happen?
Why can't I hear?
I can't feel my arm.
Is it pain or is it fear?

How did this happen?
It was a crash.
Smash, crash, bash,
Why did I crash?

How did this happen?
I think I know.
I open my eyes,
Now I know.

James Moncrieff (14)
Kirkham Grammar School, Preston

The Crash

We enter the car unknowing,
Next we know we are going,
What have we here?
The police right behind!
We really must get going,
Look out, a car in front!
We tumble once,
We tumble twice,
We have hit the car,
More than twice.
An explosion,
We're all doomed,
Everyone's out,
I can't shout,
I feel myself drifting out.

I look up,
Where am I?
The hospital, surely?
What's that monster in the mirror?
Surely it can't be my face?

Oliver Chambers (13)
Kirkham Grammar School, Preston

First Day At School

Walking to school, Dad dropped me off,
I'm starting senior school with a terrible cough.
The teacher seems nice, all bright and cheerful,
Although inside I was very scared and quite fearful.
Is she always this nice? Maybe it's because it's the first day,
I don't want to see her face in April or May.

I started my lessons, maths was up first,
There were so many rules I thought the teacher would die of thirst.
English was up next with Mrs Jones,
I don't think she liked the ringing of those new mobile phones.
It was lunchtime, a chance to get some food,
I hoped the dinner ladies were in a good mood.

After lunch I started geography, positive but full,
I tried to get in, silly me, the door was push not pull.
Next was maths again, this time in a different room,
The lesson didn't go well and I thought the teacher would go *boom*.
Now it was French, last lesson of the day,
I wanted to go early but the teacher said, 'No way!'

I'm going home now to do my homework and get some tea,
That's if I can remember where I put my house key.
Kirkham Grammar Senior School is the place to be,
That's why I know it's perfect for me.

Jake Hodgkinson (11)
Kirkham Grammar School, Preston

First Day At School

Through the gates,
Where is my map?
Left, right, left again,
How do I know that this is not a trap?

What if I get lost,
And I don't know where to go?
They say, 'Oh you'll be alright,
Just follow the flow.'

People going here and there,
So many people to have as friends,
Do my parents hope I'll get lost,
So that will be the end?

Will I forget to hand in my homework?
And if I remember, will I get it all wrong?
Red pen all over my work,
My mum says, 'Have confidence, be strong.'

How can I have confidence when I don't know where to go?
When to go and what to do there?
I'm not used to a blazer,
And all these new clothes that I have got to wear.

I wander round in circles,
And hope that I am going the right way,
I daren't ask,
I don't know what they will say.

Suddenly, a hand on my shoulder brings me back to reality,
A friendly sixth former is standing behind me.
She smiles and then shows me to my classroom,
Now I don't have to worry.

Lucy Fielding (11)
Kirkham Grammar School, Preston

My First Day At School

Feeling very nervous I knotted my new tie,
Put on my smart blazer and kissed my mum goodbye.
Waiting at the bus stop my heart was beating fast,
My first day at my new school has arrived at last.

Yelling children crowd the bus, they make an awful din,
Everyone is friendly though and I soon feel I fit in.
Unfamiliar faces are all that I can see,
My teacher is there waving, I think she's Mrs B.

She takes me to my classroom, a smile upon her face,
She makes me feel so welcome then shows me to my place.
My classmates are all friendly as nice as kids can be,
I'm sure I am going to be happy, just you wait and see.

Kerry Emmett (11)
Kirkham Grammar School, Preston

Face

She looks through watery eyes,
One stays half closed, it's discoloured and swollen.

Red shines from her cheeks,
A glistening red where the skin still weeps.

Her mouth, once smiling, is now glum,
No more smiles as the skin round her face is tight with pain.

She wears a scarf to hide her disfigurement,
But it doesn't hide the hurt in the heart.

Beautiful golden locks of hair tumble round her left shoulder,
The right side of her head bears thick brown clumps.

She has been reassured that it will grow back, that her face will mend,
But she'll never forget the accident or come to terms with her
inner feelings.

Becky Lancaster (14)
Kirkham Grammar School, Preston

My First Day At School

I got on the bus at the start of the day
Wishing my nerves would just go away
I knew exactly how big it would be
But the thought of it all just terrified me
My sister said there was no reason to worry
But I am late for reg' so I'd better hurry.

As I passed the building site
The teacher walked past and gave me a fright
As I rushed into reg', what did I see?
My teacher Miss Howe smiling at me.
We went to assembly in the multi-purpose hall,
Where the head teacher addressed us all.

We started our lesson at period four
And I am sorry to say that maths was a bore
The rest of the day was quite alright
But when I got home I got quite a fright
When I looked at my planner I was surprised to see
Just how much work was waiting for me.

Rowan Leech (12)
Kirkham Grammar School, Preston

My First Day At School

All the children are much bigger,
We look so much smaller that they might snigger.
Teenagers are running about,
And all they do is shout.
Sports, maths, English and chemistry, music, French and art,
Eight lessons a day - you'll have to be smart.

Receiving homework for a test,
Is really going to be a pest,
Luckily we'll have time to rest.
So many new teachers and so many new friends,
So many new subjects,
School never seems to end.

Jessica Hewitt-Dean (11)
Kirkham Grammar School, Preston

First Day At School

I was really excited
Couldn't wait to get started
I was a tiny bit nervous
My stomach had butterflies
So I closed my eyes
And thought of a surprise
For the day through
What would it be?
Something sweet? Something funny?
Maybe something for my mummy?
It was my dog, warm and cuddly
Now my butterflies have flown away.

Freya Mayo (11)
Kirkham Grammar School, Preston

First Day At School

F irst day at school, I was really terrified,
I did not know where anything was,
R eading and writing I really enjoy,
S tarting a new school,
T he lessons getting harder.

D ays and days of work and fun,
A ll the new pupils coming in,
Y esterday we walked around in the sun.

A ll my new friends walking with me,
T he dinners, teachers, lessons and lockers were all new to me.

S martcards and the campus were hard to figure out,
C alling and texting and using our phones at lunch all the time,
H earing the bell and rushing to class,
O ur new teachers and the new classrooms,
O ur lockers, nearly everything was different or new,
L ucia, Hannah, Cleo and me are all friends at this school now.

Charlotte Corkhill (11)
Kirkham Grammar School, Preston

My First Day At School

Everything's so big,
I'm ever so small,
I'm totally lost,
I can't find my way to the hall.

I try to do my maths,
I get into a muddle,
I go out for break,
And step into a puddle.

I go to do my English,
I do biology too,
I really need the toilet,
But I can't find the loo.

Lunch is almost over,
I go into the class,
I sit and watch the clock,
And wait for time to pass.

School is over,
But I'm a boarder, you see,
So I go and ask Matron,
What time is tea?

Christina Blenkinship (11)
Kirkham Grammar School, Preston

First Day At School

F ighting cars trying to park,
I nside it is chaos,
R oaring class bells,
S houting pupils moving quickly,
T ime for class to start.

D irty, sticky fingers from break,
A rt is next - fantastic,
Y ellow sunshine filters through the blinds.

A fter lunch it's time for rugby,
T eams and seas of navy and white.

S cience is fun to do,
C hemistry is my favourite,
H ow much longer before home time?
O nly one hour,
O nly one minute,
L et's go!

Oliver Evans (11)
Kirkham Grammar School, Preston

First Day At School

The bell was suddenly ringing
Like a harmonious choir singing
Where do I go?
Oh I don't know
Who do I ask?
It seems such a task
The older pupils are so large
They shoved and knocked and barged
Now the lessons are finally over
It's time to find my mum's old Rover.

Rebecca Eastham (11)
Kirkham Grammar School, Preston

First Day At School

Up at seven, dressed and fed, oh what a fuss!
All in order to catch that bus.
Just in time I arrive at school,
Forgot my bag, what a fool.
Full school assembly in the school hall,
All the pupils squashed in wall to wall.
Onto lessons before dinner,
The first school meal is sure to be a winner.
A few lessons more before the trip back,
Must remember tomorrow, my school rucksack.

Thomas Dewhurst (11)
Kirkham Grammar School, Preston

First Day At School

I walked through the school gate,
Not knowing what to do.
I was scared of the other children,
As they were all not new.

I walked into the hall,
And saw a very good friend,
I wasn't as scared anymore,
As she was my best friend.

I couldn't wait to see what they
Were going to do with me today,
I loved my first day at KGS,
It really was the very best.

Ellise Sewell (11)
Kirkham Grammar School, Preston

The School

K irkham Grammar is so big,
I think that teacher wears a wig,
R eading books and learning much,
K ick the ball into touch,
H omework every single night,
A rithmatic gives me a fright,
M usic is a must for me.

G eography is all at sea,
R ight away I like the place,
A rt puts paint upon my face,
M oving around every day,
M ust find a better way,
A nother building I've just found,
R ocking to a funky sound.

S coring on the hockey pitch,
C ross-country gives me such a stitch,
H istory is in the past,
O h why does time go really fast?
O ver there is the bus,
L eaving at home time is such a fuss.

Amy Parkinson (11)
Kirkham Grammar School, Preston

First Day

It's Wednesday morning, oh no, it's not!
It's the middle of the night, but no I forgot.
It's first day at Kirkham, I feel like the dead,
And Grandad is shouting, 'Get out of that bed!'
We get to the bus stop, my head just whirls,
Four people waiting, two boys, two girls.
Five minutes to bus time, that's quite a wait,
I stand there all worried, in quite a state.
One girl comes over and starts to talk,
I feel as though I just want to walk.
Although she is older, she talks for a while,
I feel a bit shy, but she's got a nice smile.
On the bus I'm alone, feeling quite flat,
Well here we are, get a grip Matt!
Out we get but where do we go?
I'll follow the rest, perhaps they all know.
Break time, lunchtime, what do I do?
Someone is coming, but who, who?
Are they talking? Yes, talking to me,
Football fans they are certain to be.
Back on the bus, thank goodness for that,
Two older boys come along for a chat.
Another boy, I found from near my home,
Not bad for a first day, after a moan.
I get off the bus, smiling slightly,
'How did it go?' Grandad asks quite brightly.
'Oh not bad,' I say, quite rueful,
Then, 'Well, pretty good if I'm being quite truthful.'

Matthew Dobbins (11)
Kirkham Grammar School, Preston

First Day At School

On my first day at school
I couldn't wait;
I was so excited as I walked
Through the gate;
I sat in reception
Waiting for Miss Glover;
It's the first day at school
Without my brother;
She showed me around
And everything was ace,
I walked into class with a smile on my face!

Nicholas Sharples (11)
Kirkham Grammar School, Preston

First Day At School

Throw on your uniform,
Jump in the car,
Run to your lesson,
Ring . . . ring . . . oh no!
The bell, I'm late.

Running to my lesson,
Where, where is the lesson?
What, what have I got?
Have I got,
Maths, English or is it biology?

What do I do?
I'm going to go home,
I'm not coming back,
I don't even know where I am?
I'm going home.

Aaron Hope (11)
Kirkham Grammar School, Preston

The Big School

Big school, this school,
I'm not fitting in at big school.
So many pupils, so many teachers,
This big place has so many features.
Vending machines and the French café,
Can't wait till Friday then it's Saturday.
Lots of homework to do tonight,
I'll be surprised if my bag goes light.
Rushing to all the classes,
Ending up with bruises and bashes.
Lockers, all the lockers, mine won't open,
Maybe the lock is twisted and broken.
We're tired, I'm tired,
Turn off our system inside that is wired.
When you're home go to sleep with a drool,
Then when you awake you'll be ready for big school.

Antonia Price (11)
Kirkham Grammar School, Preston

First Day At School

S cary at the start
C haos in the corridors
H ints when we needed help
O lder ones always there on hand
O ther friendly Year 7s of course
L oved it at last.

Jake Wilson (11)
Kirkham Grammar School, Preston

My First Day

Big people pushing by,
I tag along, not knowing
Where on earth I'm going,
Feeling a mixture of worry,
Excitement and fear.

I reach the classroom,
Lots of new faces all around,
I hear pupils chatting, making new friends,
While I stand in the corner,
Waiting for my friends to arrive.

I sit down thinking about the day,
Will it be good or bad?
What if I'm late for my first lesson?
What will they do to me?
Will they put me in *detention?*

Emma Jordan (11)
Kirkham Grammar School, Preston

My First Day At School

Endless, gloomy corridors winding like rivers.
A sea of worried faces peering into the distance.
Classrooms looming like black holes in the universe.
My heart is beating fast, I try to smile.
Kind-looking adults look down on us with care.
I begin to relax.
I spot a group of familiar faces.
New faces become friends.
The buildings lighten up.
I think I'm going to like it here.

Bethany Hiron (11)
Kirkham Grammar School, Preston

My First Day At School

The playground it's so big,
And what about the school, it's 'humungus'.
What should I do? Where should I go?
Do I look okay? Have I got this uniform on right?

Wow, this classroom's so strange,
I don't know anyone.
Will I ever make any friends?
I wish I still had my old friends.

Oh no, where's everyone going?
'Right everyone, it's assembly!'
So where do I have to go now?
I was just getting comfy.

My legs are killing me,
I've been walking from class to class,
What are they trying to do at this school,
Paralyse me?

So I've made it through the day,
Now all I need to do
Is get on the right bus!
Bus number one, that's it.

Sarah Pickford (11)
Kirkham Grammar School, Preston

Bullying

Running, running, running away,
I was surrounded on that day.
Nowhere to go, nowhere to hide,
No one there but my worst *nightmare!*
Huddled in a corner, he came over,
Followed by his mates lingering closer.
First a punch, I fell to the ground,
Then a kick and they all came round.
Getting more brutal, they started to chuckle,
It carried on through the night,
As I lost my eyesight.
Hitting, bashing, lashing, slogging,
There they left me crying, all on my own.
I couldn't wait to get home.
Seeing my family I was not
Alone.

Taibai Rankin (14)
Kirkham Grammar School, Preston

The Forest

The creaking of the trees
The crackling of the branches
The ripping of the bushes
The whispers of the night
The rustling of the leaves
The scuffling of the forest beasts
The mysterious eyes watching from the bushes
The sinister figure striding through the night
Cackling . . . creeping . . . ripping . . .

Benedict Fulford-Brown (12)
Kirkham Grammar School, Preston

The Fight And The Fright Of My Life

I was ready to fight,
He gave me a fright.
I thought he wasn't strong,
Guess I was wrong.

He was so tough,
All I could do was bluff.
His punches were like thunder,
I tried to surrender.

But he threw me in the gutter,
I tried to speak but I started to stutter.
All of a sudden I heard this thud,
And I found my face in the mud.

Yameen Shahid (13)
Kirkham Grammar School, Preston

Others . . .

Running down the alley,
My heart pounding,
My hands wet and clammy,
Beads of sweat pouring down my face,
I don't know how far it is behind me,
There could be more of them ahead,
Suddenly out of the darkness . . . blood-red eyes,
Mis-shapen figures and silhouettes,
I start to run faster,
More and more figures appear from the shadows,
They make wails like none I've heard before,
Large, black hooded creatures,
How many of them are they?
What are they?
Terror is running through my veins,
Awful, catastrophic thoughts are running through my head,
I realise that I am surrounded,
There is nowhere to run this time,
Nowhere to hide,
They have me . . .

Emily Fisher (12)
Kirkham Grammar School, Preston

Hurricane Alley

Howling, swaying, wailing, dashing,
Cold winds and rain lashing.

Debris flying everywhere,
While people just watch and stare.

Crashing of waves onto the beach,
Children stranded so no one can reach.

Trees being ripped into shreds,
Roof tiles clattering on people's heads.

The situation looking bleak,
Weather forecasts said it should be over by midweek.

Katie Gorman (12)
Kirkham Grammar School, Preston

A List Poem

I like the warm smell
of a pie hot from the oven.

I hate the stale stench
of a moth ball rotting.

I like the sight of disco lights
sparkling on the ceiling.

I hate the sight of hungry children
starving and dying slowly.

I like the cold, slippery taste
of cold juice sliding down my throat.

I like the sharp-sweet taste
of a bowl of sugar.

I like the soft touch of a leaf
cool against my leg.

I hate the slimy touch
of a rotting banana.

I like the honk
of my dad's fast car.

I hate the screeching sound
of a car coming to a halt.

Phillip Ballard (12)
Underley Hall School, Carnforth

Great Minds: Inventions

Great minds think alike,
So that's how the saying goes.
Hands and fingers go together,
So do feet and toes.

Someone invented the hoover,
Another invented the guns.
But is there any credit,
For the person who invented currant buns?

I like currant buns,
Maybe you like them too,
There are millions of inventions every day,
Like the metal machine that flew.

There's one thing about inventions that I'd really like to say,
The thing is that; they're really, really great.
But the best invention so far, that God has made,
Is my very, very, very best mate!

Tahima Ali (12)
Walshaw High School, Burnley

Food

Food comes in all shapes and sizes,
From yucky soups to sugary surprises.
Mum's home from shopping, 'What you got?' you say.
'Tomato soup,' she replies.
You yell, 'No way!'
'It's good for you. It'll help you grow.'
'Mum, my answer is no, no, no!'

Some foods are healthy, others are not,
Some foods are cold and others are hot.
Curry from the chip shop served with rice,
Spicy chicken, all sprinkled with rice.

Have you ever eaten garden peas,
Or granny apples from granny apple trees?
Baked beans are orange, they make you fart,
Wholemeal bread, it's good for your heart.

Spaghetti Bolognese all long the twirly,
It is said that bread crusts make hair curly.
I like strawberries dipped in cream,
I like chips and vanilla ice cream.

Chocolate chips in delicious brown cookies,
Get your own can of beer, for the bookies.
Marmite on bread, loved and hated,
Sweetcorn all yellow, often baited.
I like orange juice with vitamin C,
I like all foods and foods like me.

Nicola Pointing (11)
Walshaw High School, Burnley

Yummy Food

Food is something everyone eats,
From sour lemons to sweet, sugary treats.
Some are gooey like mustard and jam,
While some are straight and flat like ham.

Kids prefer the junk food, crisps and drink,
Eating healthily fruit and veg is what grown-ups think.
They eat at restaurants fish, chips and pie,
We always eat fruit and veg they lie.

Making us eat, going on a diet,
Buying low fat products causing such a riot.
At the end of the day no matter the mood,
Bread is bread, jam is jam and food is *food!*

Hira Khan (11)
Walshaw High School, Burnley

Mummy

Happy thoughts
of seeing the clown smile at the circus,
the ice cream cone with lots of sauce
and the way my mummy smiled at me.
But I still remember the bad,
the times when I did not get my own way
and when I got told off
and my mummy did not smile.

Happy thoughts
of when I got lots of sweets
and I could stay up to watch a film.
The time when I got the good badge
and the way my mummy smiled at me.
But I still remember the bad when I ate a full bag of grapes,
greedy me was sick, my daddy was not happy,
when I slammed the door in a strop
and my mummy did not smile.

Carolyn Eastwood (13)
Walshaw High School, Burnley

I Saw A Child

There was a shadow
A shadow too big to imagine
A shadow I had never seen before
As scared as I ever had been
My eyes started to fill up with water
I cried.

Ansa Jabeen (13)
Walshaw High School, Burnley

Nightmare

N ightmares are a dream
I think so anyway
'G o away!' I cried. 'Go away!'
H olding something as I lay
T ugging on my covers
M emories of the others
A nd waking up
R ealising that
E verything was just a dream.

Kelly Jane Parkinson (12)
Walshaw High School, Burnley

War

Blood and guts everywhere
Getting stuck in my hair
Dead bodies on the ground
My mate Stan has just been found
His whole body blown apart
Why oh why did this war start?
Arms and legs in the mud
Limbs from men doing the best they could
I wish this fight would come to an end
I don't want to lose anymore friends.

Domhnall McCarthy (16)
White Ash School, Oswaldtwistle

Factory Girls

The women work in the factories
So the men can all go to war
They are busy making all the bombs
Though they've never done it before

They are working in three shifts
They are working day and night
Making bombs and bullets
So the men can go and fight.

Katie Brown (16)
White Ash School, Oswaldtwistle

Time For War

The message came
Time to go to war
Back then that was the law
No time to fear
I must get my gear

I was on the front line
Next to the mine
Suddenly we were under attack
I was flat on my back
Everything went black

Bullets are flying past me
But I suddenly could not see
The memories won't fade
But have always stayed.

Ian Stocks (16)
White Ash School, Oswaldtwistle

Bullying

I don't like bullying
Especially name calling
Picking on people
Surely we are all equal.

Why pick on me?
What do they see?
Am I a weed?
Oh yes indeed.

But that's no reason
In the school season
To make me so sad
As I am the new lad.

Roy Wise (18)
White Ash School, Oswaldtwistle

Twin Towers

Twin Towers tall and straight
Wait in the sunlight for their fate
Silver aeroplanes flying in
Engines make a terrible din.

Smoke and fire, broken glass
Shattered buildings, crumbling mass
Bodies falling from a great height
I'll never forget that awful sight.

Efraz Hussain
White Ash School, Oswaldtwistle

Stammer

Why do I stammer if it's not good for me?
It sometimes makes me really sad
It sometimes makes me really mad
I've tried to talk really slow
I've tried to talk really low
People don't seem to understand
What it's like here in stammer land.

Charlotte Tolmie
White Ash School, Oswaldtwistle

A Train Ride From Colne

Taking a train from Colne to Accy
the side of the tracks looking really tacky

The railway embankment is full of junk
showing how low people have sunk

They throw their rubbish over the wall
shopping trolleys, carpets and all

Rolling along on the track
looking at houses from the back

Seeing how scruffty some gardens can be
while others are kept so beautifully

Bored youths with aerosol spray
their graffiti art is here to stay

Now spring is here with leaves so new
and all of the mess is hidden from view.

James Graham
White Ash School, Oswaldtwistle

Sadness!

My life would be gone
If I was stuck in the war
The feeling's so bad
When there are men on the floor
With guns in their hands
And bullets through their hearts
Of men being best friends and would never be apart.
The screaming and feeling of men rotting away
Is the reason why we will never forget this day.

Elizabeth Tolmie
White Ash School, Oswaldtwistle